Comparing Bugs

Bug Babies

Charlotte Guillain

Heinemann Library
Chicago, Illinois

www.heinemannraintree.com

Visit our website to find out more information about Heinemann-Raintree books.

To order:

☎ Phone 888-454-2279

🖥 Visit www.heinemannraintree.com to browse our catalog and order online.

Edited by Rebecca Rissman and Catherine Veitch
Designed by Joanna Hinton-Malivoire
Picture research by Elizabeth Alexander
Production by Duncan Gilbert and Victoria Fitzgerald
Originated by Heinemann Library
Printed and bound in China by South China Printing Company Ltd

14 13 12 11 10
10 9 8 7 6 5 4 3 2 1

Library of Congress Cataloging-in-Publication Data
Bug babies / Charlotte Guillain. -- 1st ed.
p. cm. -- (Comparing bugs)
ISBN 978-1-4329-3570-2 (hc) -- ISBN 978-1-4329-3579-5 (pb)
QL467.2.G855 2010
595.713'9--dc22
2009025553

Acknowledgments
The author and publishers are grateful to the following for permission to reproduce copyright material: Alamy p. **13** (© Nigel Cattlin); Ardea.com pp. **6** (© Jim Frazier-Densey Clyne / Auscape), **9** (© Steve Hopkin), **11** (© Auscape), **23** (© Auscape); Corbis pp. **7** (© Michael & Patricia Fogden), **17** (© Clouds Hill Imaging Ltd.); FLPA pp. **8** (© Jeremy Early), **10** (© Mark Moffett/Minden Pictures), **16** (© Gary K Smith); **22 top** (iStockphoto); NHPA pp. **4** (N A CALLOW), **14** (A.N.T. PHOTO LIBRARY); Photolibrary pp. **12** (Mark MacEwen/OSF), **18** (Martin Page/Garden Picture Library), **15** (JAMES ROBINSON/Animals Animals), **21** (Bryan Reynolds/Phototake Science), **20** (Juniors Bildarchiv), **23 top** (Mark MacEwen/OSF), **23 middle bottom** (Martin Page/Garden Picture Library); Shutterstock pp. **5** (© Cathy Keifer), **19** (© Goran Kapor), **22 left** (© Matthew Cole), **22 right** (© Vinicius Tupinamba), **23 middle top** (© Yellowj).

Cover photograph of caterpillars reproduced with permission of iStockphoto (© Simon Alvinge). Back cover photograph of a Monarch caterpillar crawling on a milkweed leaf reproduced with permission of Shutterstock (© Cathy Keifer).

The publishers would like to thank Nancy Harris and Kate Wilson for their assistance in the preparation of this book.

Every effort has been made to contact copyright holders of any material reproduced in this book. Any omissions will be rectified in subsequent printings if notice is given to the publisher.

Contents

Meet the Bugs

There are many different types of bugs.

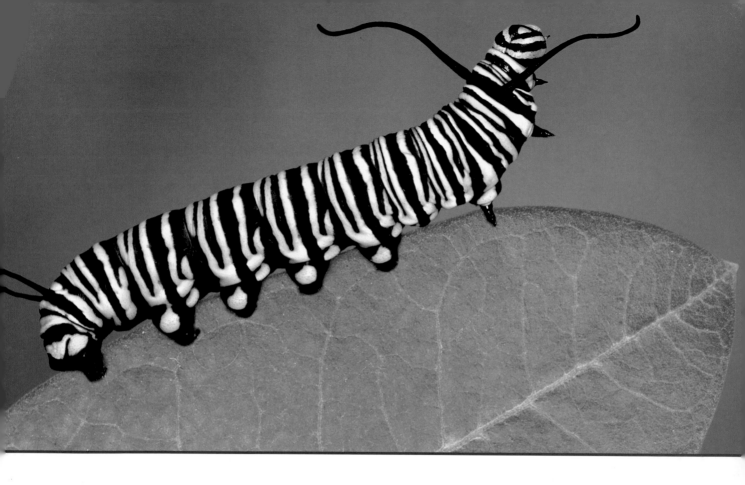

There are many different types of
baby bugs.

Eggs

egg

Some bugs lay eggs.

eggs

Butterflies lay eggs on leaves.

eggs

Mosquitoes lay eggs in water.

eggs

Flies lay eggs on food.

silk case

egg

Some spiders put a silk case around
their eggs.

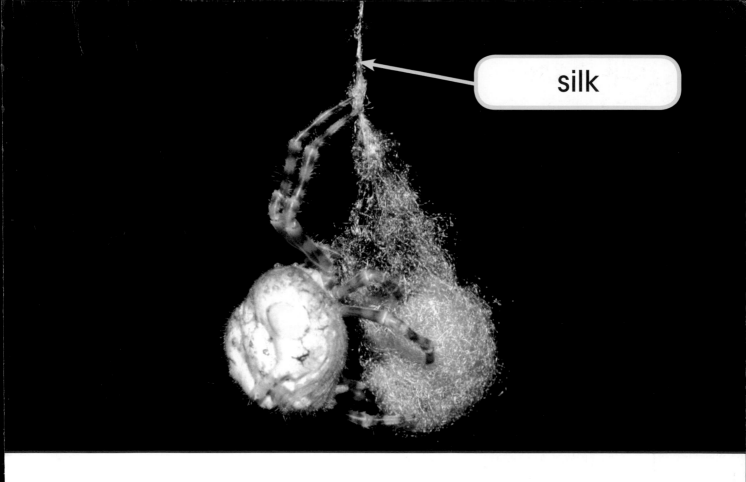

silk

Some spiders hang their eggs from a silk thread.

Bug Babies

Many young bugs hatch from eggs.

adult wood louse

young wood louse

Many young bugs look like
adult bugs.

adult centipede

young centipede

Young centipedes look like
adult centipedes.

young spider

Young spiders look like adult spiders.

Changing Bugs

young ladybug

adult ladybug

Some young bugs do not look like adult bugs.

larvae

Some eggs hatch into larvae.

egg

caterpillar

A caterpillar is a type of larva.

A caterpillar grows and changes into a butterfly.

Caring for Bug Babies

bee larvae

Some insects take care of
their larvae.

young spider

Wolf spiders carry their young on their backs.

How Big?

ladybug

mosquito

spider

Look at how big some of the bugs in this book can be.

Picture Glossary

hatch break out of an egg

insect very small creature with six legs

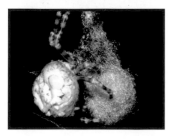
larva bug baby that hatches from an egg. It does not look like an adult. More than one is larvae.

silk soft, strong material made by spiders and other bugs

Index

Notes to Parents and Teachers

Before reading

Make a list of bugs with the children. Try to include insects, arachnids (e.g. spiders), crustaceans (e.g. wood lice), myriapods (e.g. centipedes and millipedes), and earthworms. Have they ever seen any bug eggs? Do they know what a butterfly egg hatches into?

After reading

- Get a butterfly kit for your classroom to watch how caterpillars grow and change into butterflies. Help the children to measure the caterpillars, and examine them under a magnifying glass. Ask the children to make a diary recording how the caterpillars change.
- Between spring and late summer you could go outside and hunt for bug eggs. Show the children how to look in soil, under stones, in dead leaves, and on leaves. If they find any eggs ask them to observe and record how many eggs there are, what shape and color they are, and where exactly they were found.
- If the children find any eggs you could bring them into the classroom and put them into a pot along with some of the soil or leaves on which they were found. Ask the children to watch the eggs every day and see if any bugs hatch.